FOREWORD

Good Irish tin whistle playing is characterised by smoothly-flowing melody lines, graceful ornamentation and foot-tapping rhythms. In this straightforward book you will find out how it all works. Indeed you will be given everything you need to really play the Irish whistle (except the whistle)!

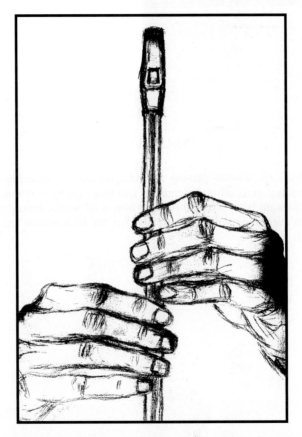

How To Play The Irish Tin Whistle
by John Ryan

1: INTRODUCTION

No one can teach you - they can only help you learn. Most things in life you have to find out for yourself and the most worthwhile things take time and practice. To learn Irish music you'll need both of these, together with a sense of fun and dedication - and sometimes a little honesty can help as well.

Unless you were (or still are) fortunate enough to learn to play at an early age I think it's fair to say that music is not always as easy to learn as some music tutors would let you believe. Human hands and fingers were well designed for grasping and holding but all hands must adapt when it comes to playing music. That's why the process takes time. True, some may appear to be better suited than others but in the end everybody has to adapt, as well as learn, in order to play.

So don't worry if at first your fingers feel uncomfortable or ill-suited to the task. With the correct understanding and practice, everyone can make good progress, especially with the Irish tin whistle. It is a wonderful instrument to learn. The wide variety of tunes and the range of sounds you can make on the Irish tin whistle will please and satisfy you for many years to come.

2: BUYING A WHISTLE

If you have just bought or are about to buy a tin whistle you can think yourself lucky. The chances are it won't even empty your pocket of change. But that doesn't mean tin whistles are cheap - it just means you're lucky! Also, as you find out more about the variety of whistles available you will probably want to try more than one kind of instrument before you find the one that is best for you. So go on, be lucky and try one or two of the many whistles available. Here are just some of the different whistles you can choose from:

1) The basic tin whistle (in Gaelic Feadóg Stáin - and no longer made of tin!) can be found in almost every gift shop in Ireland, often under the appropriate brand name Feadóg. These whistles are available in brass and nickel (actually nickel-plated over brass). The difference between the two is a matter of choice. Maybe the nickel-plated whistle has a clearer tone, maybe the brass whistle has a softer pitch!

2) Waltons of Dublin make their own range of whistles including the popular "Mellow D". This is mostly available in brass but sometimes in nickel-plate with a green mouthpiece. They also make the equally popular "little black whistle" in D.

3) Clarke's, an English company, make a range of tapered whistles. There is a model called Sweetone available in different colours. These whistles do have quite a sweet sound but I find they can be a bit "breathy" at times.

4) Oak whistles, usually made in America, are a good quality nickel-plated whistle with a black mouthpiece producing a clear, strong tone.

5) Susato are another American company that make a range of usually black, moulded plastic whistles. Although that may sound ominous, these whistles are sometimes favoured by session musicians for their clear, consistent tone and somewhat louder volume.

6) At the craft village in Dingle, Cillian O'Briaín, Uillean pipe-maker, produces an "improved" D whistle, individually voiced with a modified mouthpiece. These are nice whistles, one of my favourites. You can contact Cillian at The Craft Village, Dingle, County Kerry, Éire. Or by Fax at 353 - 66 - 9151918.

This is by no means a complete list and one or two you may have to pay for with paper money! There are also quite a lot of speciality whistles which you may discover at local craft fairs or via the Internet. And no doubt you can spend more than loose change on a hand-crafted instrument. But the whistles mentioned here are all easy to find and in my opinion, good value for money.

(Note that tin whistles are available in a number of different keys e.g. C, B flat, D. However, the most popular whistle for Irish traditional music and the one recommended to begin with here is the standard D whistle.)

Tip: You know how in life that nothing is quite perfect. Well tin whistles made in the same key will often vary slightly in pitch. To fine tune your instrument you can stand the mouthpiece end in hot water (not boiling) to loosen the join. You can then adjust the mouthpiece manually. By slightly extending or shortening the length you can lower or raise the pitch of your whistle.

3: STARTING TO PLAY

So you've bought your whistle and you're ready to play. It may be best to find a place you can relax by yourself and feel free to experiment, but if there are people around you don't worry. Take it easy! It's better to take things slowly at first.

Covering all the holes with the first three fingers of each hand while supporting the whistle on the thumbs will put you in position to play the first note of the scale. On a D whistle this will be the note D. Let your fingers relax and use the pads of the fingers rather than the very tips. Although the little fingers are never used in playing the tin whistle, I find that they can lend some support, without interfering, by resting gently against the whistle. But this is a personal thing and each player will find their own most comfortable position. When all the holes are properly covered, breathe gently into the mouthpiece and you should get a soft D note. If you have any difficulty relax, check your fingers, breathe gently and try again.

Uncovering the sixth hole by a small movement of the 3rd finger will produce the next note E. Uncovering the fifth hole gives you F# (F sharp). Uncovering the fourth hole gives you the note G. Uncovering the third hole, the note is A. Uncovering the second hole the note is B.

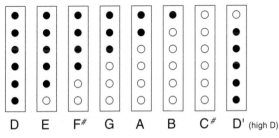

Try climbing gently up and down the scale of D.

Uncovering all the holes on a D whistle will give you the note C# (C sharp). Finally, covering all the holes again, except the first, and breathing a little harder into the whistle will give you a high D¹.

I'll confess now that while most tutors suggest that you play the high D with only five holes covered as illustrated, I learned to play it "the lazy way" with six fingers like a low D. In fact the tonal difference on my whistle is negligible.

Okay. When you are ready we can climb higher. From the high D¹ position continue the same pattern as above to give you a high E¹ (with the sixth hole uncovered), high F#¹ (two holes uncovered), high G¹, high A¹ and finally high B¹ (five holes uncovered). It is possible to play one or two notes higher than this but for our purpose, high B¹ will be our top note. (Remember that for all the high notes a slightly harder breath is required.)

I know that sometimes even a high B¹ can sound pretty shrill on a D whistle, especially when you're learning to play by yourself. It improves with time but that's the way it is. However try not to restrain your breath on the high notes as that will just produce a horrid squeak!

A WORD ABOUT KEYS

The D whistle automatically plays in the key of D and the key of D has two sharps, F# and C#, which occur "automatically" as you uncover the appropriate number of holes.

But on a D whistle you can also play in the key of G. The key of G has only one sharp, F#, and so the C has to be played as C natural.

There are two ways to play C natural on a D whistle:

1) By covering the second and third holes with your second and third fingers, thus

2) By half-covering the first hole with your first finger, thus

The second method may take a little while to get used to but it is very useful and should be learned as soon as possible. Now you can play the scale of G using either method of playing C natural:

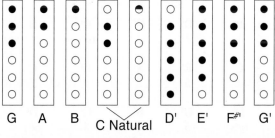

G   A   B   C Natural   D'   E'   F#'   G'

Try to practice the two methods of playing C natural until you are comfortable with both. The second method is particularly useful for faster tunes but can also be used in slow airs.

Before moving on to some real tunes in the traditional Irish music section, you might try the following exercise which together with the two previous scales of D and G, will help you become familiar with all the notes you need to play on your Irish tin whistle.

Play the following sequence to a beat of 4. The numbers beneath the notes refer to the number of holes to be covered. Again remember that the high notes marked with ' require a slightly stronger breath. The last note of each phrase is held for 2 beats.

Rhythm	1	2	3	4	1	2	3	4
	D	F#	A	D'	A	F#	D _____	
	6	4	2	6/°5	2	4	6	
	E	G	B	E'	B	G	E _____	
	5	3	1	5	1	3	5	
	F#	A	C#	F#'	C#	A	F# _____	
	4	2	0	4	0	2	4	
	G	B	D'	G'	D'	B	G _____	
	3	1	6/°5	3	6/°5	1	3	
	A	C	E'	A'	E'	C	A _____	
	2	1/2	5	2	5	1/2	2	
	B	D'	G'	B'	G'	D'	G _____	
	1	6/°5	3	1	3	6/°5	3	

Try and play the phrases smoothly one after another while keeping the rhythm at a constant tempo. When keeping time with your foot try to keep a down beat on every 1st and 3rd note. The notes in the last line are in a slightly different pattern, which simply helps to bring the sequence to a close. I've marked the fingering of the high D^I notes $6/^o5$ to indicate you can play it with either all the holes covered, 6, or with the first hole uncovered $^o5$. In faster tunes it won't make much difference but for slow airs if you get a clearer sound by uncovering the first hole then play it that way.

A NOTE ABOUT BREATHING

I suggest that you learn to breathe into the whistle without your tongue touching the mouthpiece. Later on some players may prefer to use the tongue occasionally but I recommend you first learn to let your breath flow into the whistle without obstruction. Although great reservoirs of breath are not required to play the whistle, it does seem to sound better when the breath comes from deeper down (i.e. abdominal rather than shallow breathing). Finally, many learners ask when to breathe and there is no set answer. Preferably whenever there is a natural pause in the music, but sometimes one has to take a breath where one can. Like all things it comes with practice - but it's definitely better to take breath when you need to rather than saving it up and being out of breath at the end of a tune:

"Out of breath"   *"Still breathing!"*

Next we move on to the main forms of traditional Irish music and how to play them on the Irish tin whistle.

11

4: TRADITIONAL IRISH MUSIC

Most traditional Irish music is based on the patterns of traditional dance, the best known forms being the jig and the reel. We will also look at polkas, hornpipes and slip jigs. There are many other kinds of tunes: marches, slides, set dances, slow airs and more, all of which you can play on the Irish tin whistle.

The **jig** is based on a pattern of 4 sets of 3 notes, with the stronger accent on each first note of 6, and a slightly lesser accent on the beat in between:

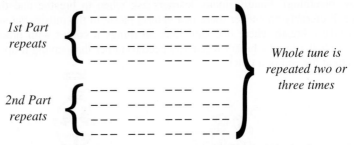

The basic jig is in two parts, each part containing 4 lines of notes on the above pattern. Each part is repeated and then the whole tune is repeated two or three times thus:

The **reel** fits together in much the same way except with the reel the basic pattern is 4 sets of four notes, with the accent on each first note of 4;

and sometimes the parts are not repeated separately - although these reels are the exceptions.

With their 3-note pattern, jigs produce a steady lilting rhythm, $\underline{1}23\ \underline{1}23\ \underline{1}23\ 123$, while the 4/4 pattern of the reel tends to deliver a more driving beat, $\underline{1}234\ \underline{1}234\ \underline{1}234\ \underline{1}234$. You could say it's the difference between rashers and sausages (--- ---) and bread and butter, bread and butter (---- ----)!

Let's try this jig titled Ryan's Favourite.

Ryan's Favourite

EAA	EAA	BAB	G_A	*(When repeating the first*
BE'E'	E'D'B	D'BA	GED	*part play the notes A_D'*
EAA	EAA	BAB	G_A	*instead of A_G)*
BE'E'	E'D'B	D'BA	A_G / A_D'	
E'_A'	A'G'E'	D'BA	G_A	*(And when repeating the*
B_E'	E'D'B	D'E'F#	G'F#G'	*second part play the long*
E'_A'	A'G'E'	D'BA	G_A	*A__ instead of A_D')*
B_E'	E'D'B	D'BA	A_D' / A__	

Then repeat the whole tune.

How did it go? Remember, it doesn't matter how slowly you go at first, but try to be sure of each note you play. Jigs don't have to be played too fast anyway in order to sound good. Tap your foot on each first note of three or if you prefer, each first note of six. If you forget the fingering for any of the notes look back at the table on page 7. And of course you remember that the high notes marked with ' are played with the same fingers as the low notes (except for D' if you prefer) but a slightly stronger breath is required.

Polkas are lively dance tunes not as difficult to accomplish as the reel and once you get the hang of them they are always good fun to play. The rhythm has more of an "up-and-down-and" feel to it!

Peig Ryan's (not all Irish tunes have Ryan in the title!)

Repeat	BDED	BDED	G_Ab	AGED	
first part	BDED	BDED	G_Ab	AGG_	*Repeat whole tune*
					at least 2 or 3
Repeat	BD'**B**g	AGED	G_Ab	AGED	*times. It's a polka!*
second part	BD'**B**g	AGED	G_Ab	AGG_	

A NOTE ABOUT TIMING

In this method of writing out tunes, a note followed by a line, G_, is twice as long as a plain G while the underlined note <u>A</u> is half as long again as a plain A. Finally the small b is half the length of an ordinary B. Keep time with your foot and I'm sure you'll get a hang out of it (as a German friend of mine would say)! I would add that my own view is not to overdo the foot-tapping. For example I often prefer to tap my foot on the first note of six in a jig. As in life, let the rhythm guide you rather than force a tune to the beat of your foot.

Hornpipes share the same 4-note pattern as reels but in the hornpipe the 1st and 3rd notes are played long while the 2nd and 4th are played short. This gives a pleasant lilt to the 4/4 rhythm and hornpipes are normally played at a slower pace than the reel.

The Clareman's Hornpipe

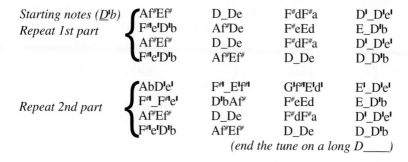

Starting notes (D'b)	Af#Ef#	D_De	F#dF#a	D'_D'e'
Repeat 1st part	F#e'D'b	Af#De	F#eEd	E_D'b
	Af#Ef#	D_De	F#dF#a	D'_D'e'
	F#e'D'b	Af#Ef#	D_De	D_D'b

	AbD'e'	F#_E'f#	G'f#E'd'	E'_D'e'
Repeat 2nd part	F#_F#e'	D'bAf#	F#eEd	E_D'b
	Af#Ef#	D_De	F#dF#a	D'_D'e'
	F#e'D'b	Af#Ef#	D_De	D_D'b

(end the tune on a long D____)

I didn't underline all the long notes (the capital letter notes) because I don't want to over-emphasise them. The strong note in each set of 4 is the first note, that's the one that should coincide with the gentle downbeat of your foot!

The **slip jig** is based on a pattern of 3 sets of 3 notes. This unusual sequence (i.e. not based on a 4-set pattern) can sometimes make these catchy tunes a little difficult to get the hang of at first. You can still tap your foot on each first note of three but remember the beat on each first note of nine and the notes will soon slip into place.

The Foxhunter (in which the sly fox slipped away)

Repeat	F#GF#	F#_D	G_E	F#GF#	F#_D	E_D
1st part	F#GF#	F#_D	G_B	AF#D	DEF#	E_D
Repeat	B_B	BAG	F#GA	B_E	EF#G	F#_E
2nd part	ABC#	D'C#B	ABC#	D'_D	DEF#	E_D

There are two more parts to this 4-part slip jig which is written out in full in the tunes section.

16

And finally the **reel**. I've left it till last because of all the different kinds of tunes I personally find it the most difficult to play. Not because it is a complicated form, far from it, but the persistent 4/4 rhythm never lets up and there are few convenient pauses to take breath. Also, reels tend to be played at a faster pace than other types of tunes and so the fingering has to be very fluent before they start to sound really good. Don't worry though, here is a good one to start you on the path. This is one of those reels where the parts are not repeated separately.

The Mountain Road

F#_AF#	BF#AF#	F#_AF#	EF#DE
F#_AF#	BF#AF#	G_F#G	EDBA
F#_AF#	BF#AF#	F#_AF#	EF#DE
F#AAA	BAF#B	ABD'E'	F#D'D'_
D'C#D'B	ADF#A	D'C#D'E'	F#G'F#E'
D'C#D'B	ADF#A	GEF#D	EDD_
D'C#D'B	ADF#A	D'C#D'E'	F#G'F#E'
D'_F#D'	AF#DF#	GEF#D	EDBA

Repeat whole tune 2 or 3 times

Remember, be sure of your notes before increasing your speed.

Now having looked at some of the popular forms of Irish traditional music, in the next section we will look at how to embellish your tunes with some graceful ornamentation.

5: ORNAMENTATION

Ornamentation is a personal thing but there are certain techniques particular to the Irish tin whistle that are worth learning properly. Once learned you will soon get used to when best to use them. Everyone develops his or her own style and no two players will ornament a tune in exactly the same way. It would be boring if they did. But the basic ornaments that players of the Irish tin whistle choose from remain the same.

Certainly one of the most useful ornaments on the Irish tin whistle is the careful use of "the cut". The cut is a very very short note played just before the main note, sometimes to punctuate the rhythm, often to break two or three notes of the same pitch. And yet the cut is so short it does not qualify as a separate note and has no time or tonal value of its own. The main difficulty in learning the cut is that although it requires a quick up-and-down movement of the 1st or 3rd finger, it is only the downward movement that produces the cut.

For example, in the opening bar of The Foxhunter there are two F sharps together:

$F^\#G F^\#$ $F^\#\_D$ G_E

In order to cut the second $F^\#$ you have to quickly raise and lower the G finger. But remember it is only the downward movement that produces the cut.

For the notes D, E, $F^\#$ and G the cut is provided by the G finger and is written thus

$^A/D$, $^A/E$, $^A/F^\#$, $^A/G$

while for the notes A and B, the B finger is used to produce a negligible C sound (actually $C^\#$) thus

$^C/A$, $^C/B$

Try the first part of The Foxhunter again including the cuts as indicated,

F#GF#	A/F#_D	G_E	F#GF#	A/F#_D	E_D
F#GF#	A/F#_D	G_B	AF#D	A/DEF#	E_D

You can also have another go at Ryan's Favourite including the cuts as indicated:

Ryan's Favourite (Jig)

EAᶜ/A	EAᶜ/A	BAB	G_A	
BEᴵᴬ/Eᴵ	A/EᴵDᴵB	DᴵBA	GED	
EAᶜ/A	EAᶜ/A	BAB	G_A	
BEᴵᴬ/Eᴵ	A/EᴵDᴵB	DᴵBA	ᶜ/A_G / ᶜ/A_Dᴵ	*(2nd time round)*
Eᴵ_Aᴵ	ᶜ/AᴵGᴵEᴵ	DᴵBA	G_A	
B_Eᴵ	A/EᴵDᴵB	DᴵEᴵF#ᴵ	GᴵF#ᴵGᴵ	
Eᴵ_Aᴵ	ᶜ/AᴵGᴵEᴵ	DᴵBA	G_A	
B_Eᴵ	A/EᴵDᴵB	DᴵBA	ᶜ/A_Dᴵ / ᶜ/A__	*(2nd time round)*

And so to "the roll". The roll is another important feature of Irish traditional music. It is often used to ornament a long note or two or more notes of the same pitch. For example to ornament three E notes with a roll the method, in slow motion, can be broken down as follows:

First play E
Then cut the E with the G finger
Then "tap" or "tip" the D hole with the third finger
i.e. E A/E D\E

Remember that with the cut it is the downward movement that produces the cut becaus we cut from a higher note to a lower one. With the "tap" it is really the upwar movement that produces the tap because we "tap" or "tip" from the note below (D\E, E\F etc.)

Cuts and taps can be tricky and it is wise to practice them separately but when practicin rolls try to think of the ornament as a whole. Because cuts and taps have no time valu the rhythmic effect of a roll should be more like - - - and not - - - - -.

The E roll: E ^{A}/E $_D$\E

The F$^\#$ roll: F$^\#$ ^{A}/F$^\#$ $_E$\F$^\#$

The G roll: G ^{A}/G $_F$\G

For the A and B roll we cut with the first finger:

A ^{C}/A $_G$\A

And for the B roll we tap with two fingers from the G hole:

B ^{C}/B $_G$\B

There is also the ornament known as "the short roll", the difference being that the sho roll begins with the cut, i.e.

The short E roll: ^{A}/E $_D$\E

The short F$^\#$ roll: ^{A}/F$^\#$ $_E$\F$^\#$ etc.

And the rhythmic effect is more like - - (hence short roll).

'The Mountain Road' which we looked at in the last section is a good example of a reel in which the short roll can be used to good effect. I've made one or two other small changes to give you an idea of how the same tune may be interpreted in different ways:

The Mountain Road (2)

S.R. F#_AF#	BF#AF#	*S.R.* F#_AF#	EF#DE	
S.R. F#_AF#	BF#AF#	*T.* G_F#G	EDBA	*S.R. = Short Roll*
S.R. F#_AF#	BF#AF#	*S.R.* F#_AF#	EF#DE	*T. = Tap*
S.R. F#AAA	BAF#B	ABD'E'	F#D'D'_	

D'C#D'B	ADF#A	D'_^/D'E'	F#G'F#E'
D'C#D'B	ADF#A	GEF#D	EDBD'
^/D'C#D'B	ADF#A	D'_^/D'E'	F#G'F#E'
D'_F#D'	AF#DF#	GEF#D	EDBD'

Tip: When playing the B note after F# you can keep the F# hole covered.

21

Because of the different rhythms of Irish music, the rhythm of the ornamenting roll can also be emphasised in different ways. In a jig for example where we want to ornament three G notes with a roll, i.e.

G ^{A}/G ₚ\G

we may emphasise the first G note as though we were playing an ordinary G followed by a short roll, thus

G ^{A}/G ₚ\G

In a reel however, the first note of a roll is generally played short.

An additional technique is the use of a roll followed by a cut. This is used where we have two or three notes of the same pitch followed by yet another note of the same pitch, as in the following jig titled 'The Boys of the Town'. We can use a roll to ornament the first three G notes followed by a cut to ornament the fourth:

The Boys of the Town

(D)G͡G͡G	^{A}/GBD^I	E^{I}D^{I}B	D^{I}BA
G͡G͡G	^{A}/GBD^I	E^{I}D^{I}B	AF$^#$D
G͡G͡G	^{A}/GBD^I	E^{I}D^{I}B	G^{I}F$^#$G^I
E^{I}D^{I}B	AGA	BGF$^#$	G_D / G_B *(2nd time)*

$\sim$ = roll

Repeat first part

D^{I}E^{I}F$^{#}$	G͡G͡G^I	A^{I}F$^#$D^I	E^{I}D^{I}B		D^{I}E^{I}F$^{#}$	G͡G͡G^I	A^{I}F$^#$D^I	E^{I}L
D^{I}E^{I}F$^{#}$	G͡G͡G^I	A^{I}F$^#$D^I	E^I_B	*2nd time play*	D^{I}E^{I}F$^{#}$	G͡G͡G^I	A^{I}F$^#$D^I	E^I_
D^{I}E^{I}F$^{#}$	G͡G͡G^I	A^{I}F$^#$D^I	E^{I}F$^#$G^I		D^{I}E^{I}F$^{#}$	G^{I}B^{IC}/B^I	F$^#$A^{IC}/A^I	E^{I}F
E^{I}D^{I}B	AGA	BGF$^#$	G_B		E^{I}D^{I}B	AGA	BGF$^#$	G_

There are many ways to use and combine rolls, short rolls, cuts and taps. The important thing is to fit your ornaments into the rhythm of the tune you are playing rather than attempt to bend the rhythm to accommodate an ornament. Sometimes a short roll will do the trick, sometimes a simple cut or tap will do.

It will help of course to listen closely to Irish music, especially any music featuring the Irish tin whistle. If you can't always attend live sessions there are plenty of tapes and CD's to choose from. See if you can tune into the rhythms of Irish music as you listen and play.

Before moving on, why not look back at The Clareman's Hornpipe and Peig Ryan's polka and see if you can ornament these tunes. Don't overdo it though. For example, Peig Ryan's may only need a cut on the double G at the end of lines 2 and 4 (i.e. AG ^{A}/G_). In The Clareman's Hornpipe you might try a roll over the 2 F sharps at the beginning of line 6 then cut the second F sharp and the second E later in the same line where there are 2 notes of the same pitch side by side. There's an obvious cut in line 2. Can you find it?

After the cuts and rolls the vibrato and slide techniques should present no problem to you. Slides are produced by sliding the fingers away from the previous note and generally from a lower note to a higher one:

For E slide from D
For F$^#$ slide from E etc.

Vibrato is a useful effect, especially in slow airs. It is produced by "wavering" a finger up and down over the appropriate uncovered hole, or holes, to give the distinctive vibrato sound:

For E use the very edge of the D hole
For F# use the D finger
For G use the E finger
For A use the D and E fingers
For B use the G finger
For C# use the A or A and G fingers
For D use breath control!

Happy wavering!

Triplets can also enhance the ornamentation of Irish music. They are usually played by adding a middle note to two notes a third or a fifth apart:

| e.g | DeF# | Ef#G | AgF# | BaG | *(a third apart)* |
| or | Df#A | EgB | BgE | Af#D | *(a fifth apart)* |

Just make sure the 3 notes fit in equally to the time of 2 notes.

Let's finish this section with a lovely slow air titled Inisheer. Don't rush it and keep a steady down beat of your foot on each 1st, 3rd and 5th note in each set of 6. I've included some possible ornamentation for the piece.

Inisheer

```
     v                   v                   v
)_) B_ C/BABDᴵ     B_ C/BABDᴵ       E_A/EBAB        D_A/DBAG
     v                   v                   v                   v
   B_ C/BABC#Dᴵ    B_ C/BABDᴵ       G_A/GBAGF#      G__DGA /G__ABDᴵ (2nd time)

      v                   v                   v                   v
   Eᴵ_A/Eᴵf#EᴵDᴵ    B_ C/BABDᴵ      Eᴵ_A/EᴵDᴵBCDᴵ    Eᴵ___BDᴵ
      v                   v                   v                   v
   Eᴵ_A/Eᴵf#EᴵDᴵ    B_ C/BABC#Dᴵ    G_A/GBAGF#      G__ABDᴵ

        v                   v                 v                   v
  d ⎧ Eᴵ_A/Eᴵf#EᴵDᴵ  B_ C/BABDᴵ      Gᴵf#EᴵDᴵBCDᴵ    Eᴵ__F#GᴵF#
    ⎨   v                   v                 v                   v
  e ⎩ Eᴵ_A/Eᴵf#EᴵDᴵ  B_ C/BABC#Dᴵ    G_A/GBAGF#      G__D_ / G____  (last time)
```

v. = vibrato

Note that the triplets in lines 3 and 5 are played with C natural i.e. half-covering the first hole only, while the triplets in lines 4 and 6 are played with C sharp (no holes covered).

Note also the longer E notes followed by a shorter f sharp. Finally it's not as complicated as it looks this one, honestly! And your effort to learn it will be well rewarded.

25

6: PUTTING IT ALL TOGETHER

Playing individual notes on the whistle is not so difficult but joining and repeating phrases of notes smoothly, with just the right amount of breath, takes time and practice. Once the individual notes of a tune have been learned it is only the constant attention to "phrasing" that brings a tune to life. Being able to do this to a foot-tapping rhythm while at the same time embellishing your tunes with some graceful ornamentation - it does take practice. Fortunately, learning Irish music on the Irish tin whistle can also be a lot of fun.

Let us look at the first part of a jig titled 'My Darling Asleep', taking the first few phrases of notes individually:

The first phrase has a starting note E^I and reads:

| (E^I) | F$^\#$D^{I}D^I | C$^\#$AA | BGG | A_G |

The second line is:

| | F$^\#$AA | D^{I}E^{I}F$^\#$ | G^{I}F$^\#$G^I | E^{I}A^{I}G^I |

Then the first phrase repeats:

| | F$^\#$D^{I}D^I | C$^\#$AA | BGG | A_G |

And finally:

| | F$^\#$AA | D^{I}E^{I}F$^\#$ | G^{I}E^{I}C$^\#$ | D^I_E^I |

Apart from the third line being a repeat of the first it's easy to see that the first half of the fourth phrase is also a repeat of the first half of the second phrase. In Irish music being able to do a good thing once is never enough! The ability to repeat a phrase fluently is itself a noble part of the art of Irish music.

As for joining, in this jig it is the last note of each line (or in the 2nd line it is the last 2 notes) that begins the next phrase, so special attention must be given to smoothly joining the lines. Then, as you know, the first part itself repeats entirely and so the last note E^l is in fact the starting note for the repeated first part. When the piece moves on to the second half this note changes so again special attention must be given to joining the two parts of the tune together. (My Darling Asleep is written out in full at the beginning of the next section). And then the whole tune repeats 2 or 3 times.

I wonder how many times the first phrase repeats through the course of this tune? But in the hands of a dedicated player each phrase will always sound fresh and vibrant, often with a slightly varied ornamentation or emphasis each time the phrase is played. Furthermore, none of the "joins" will be evident to a listener. Only the smooth transition from one part of the tune to the next.

Indeed, having mastered a number of tunes the next step is to begin joining the tunes themselves into sets of tunes. In a typical session you will usually hear two or three jigs or reels played successively. And it is one of the most exciting moments in traditional Irish music when one tune successfully breaks into another.

It only remains for me to hope you have enjoyed finding out about how to play the Irish tin whistle and I very much hope that you now have all you need to make your own progress with the tunes in the last section.

Enjoy your music.

7: A FEW GREAT TUNES

My Darling Asleep

For me, this jig has a stately feel to it and doesn't need to go too fast. I imagine the lady's golden hair strewn across the pillow in the early morning light.

(E^I)	F$^\#$D^{IA}/D^I	C$^\#$A^C/A	BG^A/G	A_G
	F$^\#$A^C/A	D^{I}E^{I}F$^\#$	G^{I}F$^\#$G^I	E^{I}A^{I}G^I
	F$^\#$D^{IA}/D^I	C$^\#$A^C/A	BG^A/G	A_G
	F$^\#$A^C/A	D^{I}E^{I}F$^\#$	G^{I}E^{I}C$^\#$	D^I_E^I / D^I_A *(2nd time)*
	F$^\#$A^C/A	D^{I}A^C/A	F$^\#$A^C/A	BAG
	F$^\#$A^C/A	D^{I}E^{I}F$^\#$	G^{I}F$^\#$G^I	E^{I}A^{I}G^I
	F$^\#$D^{IA}/D^I	C$^\#$A^C/A	BG^A/G	A_G
	F$^\#$A^C/A	D^{I}E^{I}F$^\#$	G^{I}E^{I}C$^\#$	D^I_A / D^I_E^I *(2nd time)*

End the tune by simply playing a long D instead of D^I_A or D^I_E^I.

The Butterfly

Another evocative tune, this 3-part slip jig catches the frolicking but delicate movement in flight of the wings of a butterfly.

B_E	G_E	F$^\#$__	B_E	G_E	F$^\#$ED	*} Repeat 1st part*
B_E	G_E	F$^\#$__	B_C$^\#$	D^I_B	AGF$^\#$	
B_D^I	E^I_F$^\#$	G^I__	B_D^I	G^I_E^I	D^{I}BA	*} Repeat 2nd part*
B_D^I	E^I_F$^\#$	G^I_A^I	B^I_A^I	G^I_E^I	D^{I}BA	
B_B	^{C}/B_A	G_A	B_B	^{C}/BAB	D^{I}BA	*} Repeat 3rd part*
B_B	^{C}/B_A	G_A	B_D^I	G^I_E^I	D^{I}BA	

To end the tune repeat the phrase B_E   G_E   F$^\#$__ at the end of the third part. N.B. only to end the tune.

Song of Summer
A lovely melody for every season.

(BA) G__F#	EF#GA	B_E'D'	B_AF#
G_EF#G	F#DF#G	A__B	AF#DF#
E__F#	GF#GA	B_E'D'	B_AF#
G_EF#G	AF#DF#	E_^/ED	E_BA / EF#GA
B_E'f''	E'D'BA	B_E'f''	E'D'BA
C/A_D'e'	D'BA_	BABD'E'	D'BAF#
E__F#	GF#GA	B_E'D'	B_AF#
G_EF#G	AF#DF#	E_^/ED	EF#GA / E_BA

End the tune on a long E____

The Merry Blacksmith and The Peeler's Jacket

You can play these reels one after another. The first is in the key of D, the second is in the key of G. (To recap on the system of playing the different parts of the tune correctly, the "schedule" for playing The Merry Blacksmith and The Peeler's Jacket as a pair is as follows):

The Merry Blacksmith

First Part	First Part	Second Part	Second Part
First Part	First Part	Second Part	Second Part

followed by

The Peeler's Jacket

First Part	First Part	Second Part	Second Part
First Part	First Part	Second Part	Second Part

The Merry Blacksmith

D¹_ᴬ/D¹A	BAF#A	ᶜ/ABD¹A	BAF#A
ᶜ/ABD¹E¹	F#_E¹D¹	BE¹ᴬ/E¹D¹	E¹G¹F#E¹
D¹_ᴬ/D¹A	BAF#A	ᶜ/ABD¹A	BAF#A
ᶜ/ABD¹E¹	F#A¹E¹C#	D¹BAF#	D_F#A / D_F#ᴬG¹
A¹_ᶜ/A¹G¹	F#G¹F#E¹	D¹_ᴬ/D¹A	BAF#A
ᶜ/ABD¹E¹	F#_E¹D¹	BE¹ᴬ/E¹D¹	E¹G¹F#E¹
A¹B¹A¹G¹	F#G¹F#E¹	D¹_ᴬ/D¹A	BAF#A
ᶜ/ABD¹E¹	F#A¹E¹C#	D¹BAF#	D_F#G¹/ D_F#A

End on a long D___

The Peeler's Jacket

DGᴬ/GF#	G_AG	F#GAB	C_BC
D¹G¹ᴬ/G¹F#	D¹_E¹G¹	F#D¹CA	BGAF#
DGᴬ/GF#	G_AG	F#GAB	C_BC
D¹G¹ᴬ/G¹F#	D¹_E¹F#G¹	F#D¹CA	BGGG / BGD¹E¹F# (S.R.)
G¹G¹G¹F#	D¹_E¹F#	G¹F#G¹A¹	B¹G¹A¹F#
G¹G¹G¹F#	D¹_E¹F#G¹	F#D¹CA	BGD¹E¹F#
G¹G¹G¹F#	D¹_E¹F#	G¹F#G¹A¹	B¹G¹A¹F#
G¹B¹A¹G¹	F#D¹ᴬ/D¹E¹	F#D¹CA	BGD¹E¹F# / BGᴬ/G_

Remember where there are two endings indicated at the end of a part, you play the first ending the first time round and the second ending the second time round.

...coat Loose and **Pipe on the Hob**

...e pair of jigs in the key of G. Play them quite lively one after another and imagine
...you will. The most obvious cuts have been left out.

...coat Loose

(CA)	GEE	CEE	GEE	G_A
	GEE	CBC	AD$^{I\!A}$/D^I	^{A}/D^{I}CA
	GEE	CEE	GEE	G_G^I
	F$^{\#}$E^{I}D^I	CAG	AD^{I}C$^{\#}$	D^{I}CA / D^{I}E^{I}F$^{\#}$

	$\widetilde{G^IG^IG^I}$	^{A}/G^{I}E^{I}D^I	CAB	C_D^I
	E^{I}A^{IC}/A^I	G^{I}E^{I}D^I	E^{I}A^{IC}/A^I	G^{I}E^{I}F$^{\#}$
	$\widetilde{G^IG^IG^I}$	^{A}/G^{I}E^{I}D^I	CAB	CD^{I}E^I
	F$^{\#}$E^{I}D^I	CAG	AD^{I}C$^{\#}$	D^{I}E^{I}F$^{\#}$ / D^{I}CA

End tune on a long D___

...on the Hob

...D^I	A_G	$\widetilde{F^{\#}F^{\#}F^{\#}}$	DED
...:	CBC	E_D	^{A}/DF$^{\#}$A
...B	CBA	BAG	$\widetilde{AAA}$
...:	CBC	E_D	^{A}/DF$^{\#}$A / D_E^I

...F$^{\#}$	D^{I}C$^{\#}$D^I	F$^{\#}$_D^I	^{A}/D^{I}C$^{\#}$D^I		$\widetilde{F^{\#}F^{\#}F^{\#}}$	D^{I}C$^{\#}$D^I	F$^{\#}$_D^I	^{A}/D^{I}C$^{\#}$D^I
...B	C_D^I	E^{I}D^{I}E^I	A^{I}G^{I}E^I	*2nd*	E^{I}D^{I}B	C_D^I	E^{I}D^{I}E^I	A^{I}G^{I}E^I
...F$^{\#}$	D^{I}C$^{\#}$D^I	F$^{\#}$_D^I	^{A}/D^{I}C$^{\#}$D^I	*time*	$\widetilde{F^{\#}F^{\#}F^{\#}}$	G^{I}F$^{\#}$G^I	A^{I}G^{I}F$^{\#}$	G^I_E^I
...E^I	A^{I}G^{I}E^I	^{A}/E^{I}D^{I}C$^{\#}$	D^I_E^I		F$^{\#}$E^{I}D^I	E^{I}A^{I}G^I	E^{I}D^{I}C$^{\#}$	D^I__

Note the occasional C sharps in these tunes in the key of G.

John Ryan's

Another Ryan! And not me. I had to include this polka though. It's a great little tune and featured in that great little movie "Titanic". Don't stop till you drop.

D'_D'_	BC#D'B	A_F#_	A_F#_
D'_D'_	BC#D'B	A_F#_	E_D_
D'_D'_	BC#D'B	A_F#_	A_D'E'
F#_D'_	E'_C#_	D'___	D'___ / D'_D'E'
F#_D'_	A/D'_E'F#	G'_F#_	E'_D'_
F#_D'_	A_D'_	F#_G'_	A'_D'E'
F#_D'_	A/D'_E'F#	G'_F#_	E'_D'_
F#_D'_	E'_C#_	D'___	D'_D'E'/ D'___

Tap your foot on each first note of 4 to get this one moving or if you prefer, each first note of 8.

Drowsy Maggie

Also features in "Titanic". An ironic title as this reel never stops either! Like 'The Mountain Road', the parts are not repeated separately.

S.R. E_BE	DⁱEBE	*S.R.* E_BE	AF#DF#
S.R. E_BE	DⁱEBE	BABC#	DⁱAF#D
S.R. E_BE	DⁱEBE	*S.R.* E_BE	AF#DF#
S.R. E_BE	DⁱEBE	BABC#	DⁱAF#A
Dⁱ_F#Dⁱ	C#DⁱEⁱC#	DⁱEⁱF#Dⁱ	F#AⁱC/AⁱF#
Dⁱ_F#Dⁱ	C#DⁱEⁱC#	BABC#	DⁱAF#A
Dⁱ_F#Dⁱ	C#DⁱEⁱC#	DⁱEⁱF#Dⁱ	FⁱAⁱC/Aⁱ_
BⁱGⁱAⁱF#	GⁱEⁱF#Dⁱ	BABC#	DⁱAF#D

Repeat whole tune 3 or 4 times

End the tune by adding a long E_____

Tip: When playing the B notes after E you can continue to cover the 4th and 5th holes. (It's quicker that way and Maggie won't mind!)

The Foxhunter

Here it is again with the four parts. In this slip jig the third part is a repeat of the first but is played in the higher octave.

F#GF#	A/F#_D	G_E	F#GF#	A/F#_D	E_D	} *repeat 1st part*
F#GF#	A/F#_D	G_B	AF#D	A/DEF#	E_D	

B͂_B	C/BAG	F#GA	B_E	A/EF#G	F#_E	} *repeat 2nd part*
ABC#	DᴵC#B	ABC#	Dᴵ_D	A/DEF#	E_D	

F#GᴵF#ᴵ	A/F#ᴵ_Dᴵ	Gᴵ_Eᴵ	F#GᴵF#ᴵ	A/F#ᴵ_Dᴵ	Eᴵ_Dᴵ	} *repeat 3rd part*
F#GᴵF#ᴵ	A/F#ᴵ_Dᴵ	Gᴵ_Bᴵ	AᴵF#Dᴵ	A/DᴵEᴵF#ᴵ	Eᴵ_Dᴵ	

GᴵF#Eᴵ	DᴵC#B	AGF#	B_E	A/EF#G	F#_E	} *repeat 4th part*
ABC#	DᴵC#B	ABC#	Dᴵ_D	A/DEF#	E_D	

Frankie Kennedy's

A favourite reel. Frankie Kennedy, one of Ireland's best-loved musicians.

AEᴵA/EᴵDᴵ	Eᴵ_EᴵF#	GᴵEᴵF#Dᴵ	EᴵDᴵBG
AEᴵA/EᴵDᴵ	Eᴵ_EᴵF#	GᴵEᴵDᴵB	C/BAC/AG
AEᴵA/EᴵDᴵ	Eᴵ_EᴵF#	Gᴵ_F#Gᴵ	EᴵF#GᴵEᴵ
Dᴵ_EᴵF#	Gᴵ__Eᴵ ___	DᴵBC/BA	C/A__G / A____

Aᴵ_EᴵF#	Gᴵ_GᴵF#	GᴵEᴵF#Dᴵ	EᴵF#Gᴵ_
Aᴵ_EᴵF#	GᴵEᴵCEᴵ	A/Eᴵ_DᴵB	C/BAC/A_
Aᴵ_EᴵF#	Gᴵ_GᴵF#	Gᴵ_F#Gᴵ	EᴵF#GᴵEᴵ
Dᴵ_EᴵF#	Gᴵ_GᴵEᴵ	A/Eᴵ_DᴵB	C/BAC/A_ / C/BAC/AG

End tune on C/BAC/A_

Watch out for the C natural in line 6.

Merrily Kiss the Quaker

This last tune is a 3-part slide and like the jig, the slide has a basic pattern of 4 sets of 3 notes. However the result is a little different as you will see. There's still a beat on each first note of three but, in the first part, there's an extra emphasis on the two C notes for example. Take it from there and play it with a little bit of oomph! There's plenty of cuts and rolls to keep the dancers on their toes.

AB	DGB	C_A	BGE	GAB	DEG	A͡A	ᶜ/AGE	*repeat*
AB	DGB	C_A	BGE	GAB	D_E	G͡G	ᴬ/G_D / ᴬ/G_A	*1st part*
GᴬG	AGᴬG	BGᴬG	AGE	GAB	DEG	A͡A	ᶜ/AGA	*repeat*
GᴬG	AGᴬG	BGᴬG	AGE	GAB	D_E	G͡G	ᴬ/G_A / ᴬ/GBDꞌ	*2nd part*
GꞌG͡ꞌGꞌ	AꞌGꞌAꞌ	BꞌGꞌEꞌ	DꞋBDꞌ	GꞌG͡ꞌGꞌ	ᴬ/GꞌAꞌBꞌ	Aꞌ__	ᶜ/AꞌGꞌF♯	*repeat*
AꞌGꞌ	F♯GꞌF♯	EꞌF♯Eꞌ	DꞌBA	GAB	D_E	G͡G	ᴬ/GBDꞌ / G_D	*3rd part*

End the tune on a long ᴬ/G__

You may even find a note or two to slide off when you're into the swing of this one. The dancers are waiting. Have fun and enjoy!